Reading-Based Writing

TITLES OF RELATED INTEREST

College Writing Basics, Fourth Edition, Thomas E. Tyner (1996)

Composing Through Reading, Second Edition, Peter Elias Sotiriou (1994)

Critical Thinking: Reading and Writing in a Diverse World, Second Edition, Joan Rasool, Caroline Banks, and Mary-Jane McCarthy (1996)

Critical Thinking and Writing: A Developing Writer's Guide with Readings, Kristan Cavina (1995)

Developing Writers: A Dialogic Approach, Second Edition, Pamela Gay (1995)

Inside Writing: A Writer's Workbook, Form A, Third Edition, William Salomone and Stephen McDonald (1996)

Inside Writing: A Writer's Workbook, Form B, Second Edition, William Salomone, Stephen McDonald, and Mark Edelstein (1994)

Making Connections Through Reading and Writing, Maria Valeri-Gold and Mary P. Deming (1994)

Patterns and Themes: A Basic English Reader, Second Edition, Judy R. Rogers and Glenn C. Rogers (1996)

The Research Paper, Seventh Edition, Audrey Roth (1995)

Texts and Contexts: A Contemporary Approach to College Writing, Second Edition, William Robinson and Stephanie Tucker (1994)

Views and Values: Diverse Readings on Universal Themes, Kari Sayers (1996)

Writing as a Life-Long Skill, Sanford Kaye (1994)

Writing Paragraphs and Essays: Integrating Reading, Writing, and Grammar Skills, Second Edition, Joy Wingersky, Jan Boerner, and Diana Holguin-Balough (1995)

Writing Voyage: A Process Approach to Basic Writing, Fourth Edition, Thomas E. Tyner (1994)

Writing with Writers, Thomas E. Tyner (1995)